THE OFFICIAL WOMEN'S GUIDE ON HOW A MAN SHOULD CHEAT

SIX FERNANDEZ

Library of Congress Cataloging-in-Publication Data has
been applied for.

ISBN 13: 978-0-578-03 195-8

FIRST EDITION

10 9 8 7 6 5 4 3 2 1

This book is dedicated to anyone who has ever dared to dream. Sometimes in life you can't sit around and wait for "opportunity" to come knocking, sometimes you have to get up and ring the doorbell yourself!

THE OFFICIAL WOMEN'S GUIDE ON HOW A MAN SHOULD CHEAT...

TABLE OF CONTENTS

Note to the female reader

Note to the female reader:

Allow me to start by saying to the women THIS BOOK IS NOT FOR YOU!

This book is for men... *now with that being said...*

I am sure you took one look at the title of this book and thought "How could you write this?"

Let me be 100% real in saying there is no way I couldn't. We have all been in relationships where we were crushed and heartbroken to find out that our man had cheated on us. We have all wondered how we could have been so naïve to be so fooled. I also understand that many women will look at the title and think "my man would never cheat on me" if so, I am especially talking to you!

I felt it was appropriate for me to explain my motivation for writing this guide. Relationships these days go one of two ways, you are either being cheated on or being cheated with. I also understand that we as women can influence and encourage our men to cheat on us! Isn't it funny that we will say to our men "You should find one of them weak ass girls out there that you can run, because there is NO WAY I am going to shut up and let you run me!" The next thing you know your man is coming home late and leavin' early, because he has set out to do just that!

Women also don't do a good job of keeping our men fed and sexually satisfied. We complain too much, talk too much, nag too much, are too tired far too much, and cling on too much! (I have been friends with many of you women, ya'll have made me press the ignore button on my cell phone too.) Women have so much drama about us. No man in America wants to deal with the job politics that comes along with "working for the man", and then have to come home to "Why didn't you take the trash out?" "When you gon' mow the lawn?" "Take the dog for a walk." "My car needs an oil change."

We make our men want to be anywhere but at home with us. We are also notorious for getting a man, and thinking the game we ran to get him will be enough to keep him forever with out any additional maintenance. Men have complained about this for ever. Men will tell you how their woman cooked, cleaned, catered to them, and sexed them down in the beginning. After the man was hooked, the closest thing he'd get to a home cooked meal was a peanut butter and jelly sandwich!

So with all that being said men are going to cheat bottom line, and it's about time I taught them how! We can all agree that cheating is a "game", however never before has this game been so well defined- until now. Never have there been guidelines and rules- until now. Though the pages of this guide I will teach men who to cheat with and how, the best times of day to cheat, positions, excuses, and most importantly how to be a successful cheater without being caught!

So let me guess, you hate me and my stupid little guide- fine with me, don't buy the book. But when all of a sudden your man who previously couldn't even look in the direction of another woman without being caught, now has you thinking your last threat of leaving has him faithfully committed, don't believe it girlfriend! While your ass was busy hatin' on me, your man was obviously busy reading my book!

CHAPTER 1- GETTING STARTED

Congratulations, you purchased the book. Whether you feel you're a rookie or an old pro (and can use no pointers when it comes to cheating) it doesn't really matter. Even if you have cheated 100 times or never at all you will be able to take something away from this book that will improve your game!

I am not sure if there is an exact science to cheating; however through the pages of this book you will be able to avoid most of the silly little things you men do that get you caught time and time again. I, as well as many of the other women I've surveyed feel the offense is not the act of cheating, it's the confirmation and the fact that our men cheated and **got caught** that causes the problem.

Let's talk about why you men cheat in the first place. One of the main issues is that women don't know their place. Women have too much mouth, and too little respect. We cling, we whine, we bitch, we are never satisfied, and quite frankly we talk entirely too much!

Us women always gotta have the last word, always wanna argue, never wanna let an issue go, and always gotta be right.

We don't do a good job in the kitchen either. In the beginning we were cooking, baking, frying, broiling, sautéing, and flaying. We always had hot meals on the table and sweet desserts in the fridge.

The minute we get ya'll ass- the kitchen is officially CLOSED. You'd have a better chance at getting them to drop Michael Vick's charges than getting your woman to cook so much as a bag of popcorn without hearing a whole lot of lip!

We also do a half assed job in the bedroom. In the beginning, we would go out of our way to "woo" a man, always looking and smelling nice, always well groomed, in shape, very polite, never *really* hungry, and calling here and there or days apart.

Never really needy at all, and when it came to sex, we would ride that ass like our name was Amtrak!

But the minute you wife us you would think we were one of the seven dwarfs. If you can catch us on a day when we are not too sleepy, grumpy, crampy, dopey, drowsy, tired, or full of I don't give a damn, you might just get some.

Now you know as well as I do, when you do get some, it's drier than the Sahara Desert. You try to get the party started but the only position you can get her to lay in is the same position she sleeps in.

After all of that effort and the fact that you are still not satisfied, you are then forced to "superman that hoe" which being since she is fast asleep and has been for some time, seems like the natural thing to do!

Now after you start claiming our ass as yours the **"REAL US"** comes out, and we go all the way crazy! We start calling every hour on the hour, several times an hour. We always got something to say, and you can't even walk in the bathroom anymore without seeing a douche bag, weave tracks, or make-up, etc thrown or draped somewhere.

We pack away our sexy little thongs and pull out our granny panties/ period draws. We always need something- hair done, nails, toe nails, gas money, eyebrow waxed, you name it, we need it!

We also seem to triple in price! When you first met us we were the quiet, cute chick who ONLY wanted a salad. Now we are the loud mouth hungry bitch who is ordering appetizers, desserts, full size entrees, and cussing out the waitress for cooking our filet mignon too long!

Women are also notorious for barking orders. We go from "honey, can you please bring me a drink of water?" to "Get me some water, and I need plenty of ice too!" "Not the little chips of ice you brought me last time." "And I need a big glass, I told you I don't drink out of plastic cups!" "Make sure you rinse out the glass, you know our baby don't be washin' the dishes clean, and start the dish washer while you at it." "Don't forget to turn off the kitchen light either and double check the back door, I don't want anybody to come in here on us!"

Hell, by this time you are thinking if anybody did come in to please kill you first because this bitch is making you want to kill yo' damn self! Meanwhile back at the ranch, you ask her for one simple little thing and she has all kinds of reasons why she can't assist you. You ask her for a CUP of water, she'll reply "What's wrong with you, yo feet broke?" "I ain't yo' slave, I'm not going that way!"

Things with us women just aren't ever equal, and men you already know what will happen if you lose your job! As long as you were working your woman referred to things as "our house" "our kids" "our credit" "our cars" "our life", but the very minute you come home unemployed everything changes (men you know I ain't lying). It then becomes "Where you need to go in my car?" "Why you got all these lights on in my house" "yo' broke ass is about to ruin my credit" "my kids need some new clothes!"

And if you have kids that's a whole nother story! Everything becomes "Go ask your daddy!" Not only do you have to deal with her nagging ass on days you'd just assume be invisible, you now have to deal with these little nag maggots in training. Now, don't get me wrong I know you love your kids, but having to deal with them and their mother is a lot of work.

Upon your key unlocking the door, it's "Daddy" "Daddy" "Daddy" nonstop! You can't even unwind, without hearing your woman say, "I'm tired now, it's your turn!" Never mind the fact that you have just had the day from HELL!

The point in all of this is sooner or later you have or will encounter the thought that the grass could possibly be greener on the other side, and while you may not want to trade in your grass for some of that artificial turf just yet, you at least wouldn't mind playing on it for a while.

I would like to say men generally do not sit around and say, "You know what, today seems like a good day to start cheating!" and then seek out to do so, **but you should**! This is a major decision that should not be done impulsively!

You should **NOT** see an attractive or "easy" woman and say, "why not?" This is the wrong thing to do, and it will lead you to a place of headache and pain
<u>GUARANTEED!</u>

There are rules to playing this game, and it's about time you found out just what they are!

CHAPTER 2- RULE #1- MAKING SURE YOU SUIT UP

As you continue to read you should start to notice the use of football terms. In doing so I wanted to be able to communicate to you in terms that you could relate to!

The first term you should be familiar with is "suiting up". In the game of football you are not going to be able to properly play a full contact sport **PROFESIONALLY** unless you do so.

You will need to make sure that every pad is in place to avoid serious injury and/ or bodily harm. Now we all know suiting up will not **GUARANTEE** you will always be injury free, but it will lessen the chance of long term harm and pain.

The same holds true in this situation. One of the most common reasons men get caught is that they were out playing the game and were not properly suited.

Always, always, always **USE** a condom! I don't care if you have been cheating for 1 day or 365 days, use one anyway. The day you decide to have sex without wearing your suit, you need to stop cheating on the one you were cheating on, and start cheating on the chick you use to cheat with. Meaning it's time to pack it up and move it out.

It's simple, suiting up will lessen the chance of pregnancy or sexually transmitted diseases, both of which will lead to you getting caught and your woman will find out. Remember, you are in control of your team at all times!

I like to think about it like this, you are the Quarterback. Your wife/ girlfriend and kids are your team. You are responsible for them and the safety of them at all times *especially* while you are out in the field.

The opposing team is the rest of the world, and all the things in it, bills, debt, your boss, etc. You need to make sure you and your team continues to make forward progress down the field by avoiding the tackles, or pitfalls of the opposing team. Your touchdowns are things like your house, car, job, savings, 401k, happiness, and things like this.

Now while some teams can score all by themselves, many times in order to out score your opponent you may need a little assistance. Sometimes you as the Quarterback may have to bring in the kicker to help you. The "Kicker" in this book is the woman you decide to cheat with. She should be able to come in and kick whenever needed. In this case "kick" means have sex.

Meaning she is not your full time woman, and should know her position! She should know that you have no intention to use her or need her for anything besides kicking.

You need to make sure you are **100% HONEST** with your "Kicker" at all times.

When you feel like having some stress free sex or fun, you call her. When you want somebody to shut up and listen, you call her. When you want to be pampered, and made to feel like the man you truly are, you call her.

An important rule for you to also remember is that she should **NEVER** tell you when to put her in the game! She should know to always be ready and waiting to kick for you when ever you call!

Outlining these rules to your "Kicker" should even help you avoid playing without your suit. Even your "Kicker" should know to have a few spare suits ready at your disposal!

It is however important to note if you do use a suit that your "Kicker" provides always examine it carefully for any rips, tears, or puncture marks. You should also **NEVER** allow your "Kicker" to put your suit on for you! *(Hey you can never be too sure)*

You will need to be cautious at all times! You will also need to remember you should never be willing to trade your "Kicker" for your whole team. If she is not ready to kick off to your rules, it's simple…**TRADE YOUR "KICKER" FOR A NEW ONE!** Whether you know it or not there are plenty "Kickers" to choose from.

You should also know in the game of football the kicker doesn't even practice with the rest of the team. Normally while the team is practicing or playing the kicker can be found off to the side quietly practicing the kick, or getting ready to!

Meaning your "Kicker" should always be an extension of your team, never give the "Kicker" a reason to be *apart of it!*

I can't tell you the number of men who had babies by a woman they cheated with. The men never had any intention on being with them for real. Now not only do these men have to deal with these women, but the woman they really wanted to be with is long gone.

Now in some scenarios the men were actually able to keep their team together, but the child by the woman they cheated with always seems to suffer. There is always some level of resentment towards the child, normally from the wife/girlfriend.

I would also like to remind you of another important fact. While you are out cheating without using a condom, you have no idea what the woman you are cheating with may have or has had.

Anything you get you stand the chance of giving this to your home team. We all know the risks; ask yourself, do you want to give your woman a disease. Do you want to risk her life *and* yours?

Playing the field can be one of the best things or one of the worst. Always know the rules, always find players who will play by them, and always wear a condom. No sex in the world is worth not wearing one!

CHAPTER 3- RULES TO PLAYING THE FIELD

Now in the last Chapter we discussed the most important rule of all which is wearing a condom at all times, and although this is the **most** important rule, it's not the **ONLY** rule.

Messing around and cheating is two totally different things! Messing around is flirting, getting phone numbers, going out with your friends to the clubs and buying women drinks, things like this. When you cheat you have to make sure it's done by the book, **this book!**

Before finding a "Kicker" to add as an extended player of your team, you need to know this, there are some women out there who **ONLY** date men who already have a woman.

I have found many women do so because they feel it's easier to borrow a man some of the time than to have a man all of the time. They feel this way because they don't want a full time relationship, with commitments, and obligations. They want to be able to come and go and do as they please.

Then there is another kind of woman. This other kind of woman wants an already taken man so that she can take him for herself! These kinds of women are willing to do so by any means necessary! Even if it means punching holes in the condom, using a turkey baster, or lying by saying they can't get pregnant, when they know they can. This type will seek and destroy lives, just to take another woman's man.

Women are cunning characters! Think of the biblical downfalls, in many cases women were the cause. No matter how long you have known them, how much you have in common, or how perfect she appears, there is no sure fire way to be able to tell what kind of "Kicker" you have, so always air on the side of caution!

In an effort to help you avoid some of the pitfalls that are easy to get caught up in, here are a list of rules to live by when selecting your "Kicker" in no particular order...

Rule #1-

NEVER PICK A "KICKER" WHO HAS KICKED IT WITH YOUR WOMAN OR HOME TEAM

If she knew/ knows who your woman is - don't do it. You will get caught!

I have seen this time and time again. Everything was going fine and your woman's friend (who you've been cheating with) decides she needs to come clean with her friend. Or if they use to be friends and aren't any longer this is even worse. Not only will you find yourself in a situation where if you stop cheating she will surely tell but she just may do so anyway. Many women will cheat with their past friends' man only to get back at their past friend!

NEVER choose a "Kicker" who knows your children. This includes your child's teacher, your child's friend's mother. Also do not "kick" with someone who went to school with your woman or your woman's past or present co-worker. You need to find someone who doesn't know your woman or family. You never want your "Kicker" to be able to have any direct contact with your family, or woman.

RULE# 2-

NEVER TAKE YOUR "KICKER" HOME OR LET HER KNOW WHERE YOU LIVE OR WORK

Here again you will get busted!

It seems so easy to invite her over especially when your woman/ family are out of town. It seems harmless right; I mean what the worst that could happen?

Well let's see here, have you considered she may return when your wife/girlfriend *is* home. What if you break it off with her? Your "Kicker" will have enough information to cause a problem or at the very least some questioning from your wife/girlfriend.

Some women are so cold they will purposely leave things like strands of hair, hair accessories, under garments, tampons, etc; behind just so it can be found.

One woman shared with me that she once was taken to the house and left unattended long enough to go through find the wife's panty drawer. She then took her panties off and mixed them in with the wife's. Now let me be the first to say, I don't care if your woman has **1000** pairs of panties, she will notice the **ONE** pair that is **<u>NOT</u>** hers!

Another woman shared with me (while I was writing this book) that she and a group of friends would cheat with married men. They would get invited to the house when the wives were out of town. While they were there they would grab junk mail (like an advertisement) and put it in their purse.

(She said the men would *just* give the directions on how to get to their house, but would never give the full address.)

Once she said she was left alone long enough to go through some of the drawers in his bedroom. When she came across the wife's drawer she took one of the wife's bras and put it in her purse.

When times were good, life was great. However the minute their relationship was over she gift wrapped the wife's bra and addressed it **TO: Mrs. (his last name)**. She then shipped it overnight delivery back to his house (thanks to the junk mail she took, it had his full address). She said she attached a note to the wife's bra that read...

"I apologize, I must have grabbed this by mistake the other night when I was at your house fucking your man, my bad!"

Now if what you've just read is not enough to convince you to **NEVER** take your "Kicker" to your house, then you are clearly hopeless and destine for trouble! I will leave you with this, my momma use to say "the easiest way is the best way," and not taking your "Kicker" home after reading this is clearly best!

RULE #3-

NEVER FOR ANY REASON GIVE YOUR "KICKER" MONEY

This is the *"golden rule"* and it **MUST** be followed at all times. Giving money to your "Kicker" is **TROUBLE** with a capital **T**!

First off by doing so you are changing the game, you are also letting your "Kicker" have more power than she ever should. If you are utilizing your "Kicker" as you should be, your "Kicker" should never feel comfortable enough to even ask or imply she needs cash.

Think about it this way, if all of a sudden a stray cat starts meowing on your door step and you start feeding it and giving this stray cat milk, that stray cat that you thought was just going to eat and be on it's way is now there for ever. Even if it leaves for a while, sooner or later it will come back for more.

These women are the same way. The minute you start giving them money they will not only keep coming back, but most importantly it will be harder for them to leave when you want them to. They will become dependent. Dependency soon bring desperation, meaning they will connive, lie, even steal to keep that level of comfort you have now started providing.

Let me also explain this includes purchasing anything over **$20** (and that's pushing it). I know this may sound cheap, but your

"Kicker" should not expect for you to purchase a manicure, groceries, or even a bag of hair weave.

Train her early by not allowing her to feel comfortable enough to even ask for a hot meal. You can do this by reminding her, this is sexual, not financial or personal.

Speaking of meals, I need to tell you why restaurant style dining is a big **"no-no"**! Not only do you run the risk of being caught, but you are sending the message that you care enough about her to *risk* being caught.

A general rule of thumb is if it **can't** be purchased through the drive thru then it shouldn't be purchased at all!

If it **can** be purchased through the drive-thru, it should always be purchased by you! **NEVER** physically hand money to your "Kicker"!

Even if your "Kicker" drove, and you are sitting right next to her, lean past your "Kicker" and hand it to the drive-thru window employee- **YOURSELF!** By handing money to your "Kicker" this will confuse her and make her think you care more about her than you really do. Likewise, if you take her through a drive-thru window and you spend $5.39; do not give her the $14.61 change. Remember spending $20 *(on rare occasions)* is the maximum you should ever spend. It's preferred you spend nothing at all!

If you think about making one purchase outside of these guidelines or want to consider giving your "Kicker" a small minimal amount just this one time- **don't do it!** By doing so you are starting a pattern that your "Kicker" will not want broken.

CHAPTER 4- THE BEST FIELDS TO PLAY, BEST TIMES, AND FORMATIONS

Okay so you have identified your "Kicker", or have you?

Let's discuss *"The Best Fields to play on"*. To make this actually work your "Kicker" will need to have her own field, meaning her own house or apartment.

The biggest reason is this will prevent her from wanting to come over to your place. Not to mention her place is somewhere you can come in and out as you please. This is also a place that can be readily available at a moments notice.

I have seen time and time again. The "Kicker" does not have her own spot to kick it, next thing you know the man wants to have sex so badly that he gets sloppy, gets a hotel room and gets caught. Even if you pay cash for it it's still too risky. Not to mention if you followed the rule of not spending over $20 on your "Kicker" this will pretty much cancel this option.

I also had a woman share with me that she cheated with a married man, who got an apartment for her in his name. Not only is this the dumbest thing I've ever heard, but by doing so you are screaming "Catch me now, I wanna be caught!"

Bottom line, you need to learn how to avoid any unnecessary risk, and by your "Kicker" having her own house or apartment this can be easily avoided.

Okay I think you got that one. Next let's discuss the best time to cheat, and yes there is one.

I like to call it **"ON PEAK *vs.* OFF PEAK"**. You know how your cell phone plan will give you a time range when it's free to talk and then another time range when it's not; well this has the same premise.

Your **ON PEAK** time in this case will be the hours of which you work. Your **OFF PEAK** is when you are **OFF**. So say for example your work schedule is *Monday through Friday 8am to 5pm,* these are the hours you should cheat. If you work a night shift, same thing, when you are off cheating is **prohibited**, and while it can be done, remember the easiest way is still best.

Cheating during **ON PEAK** hours is truly easy. You have your lunch break, client meetings, etc. I also have adjusted this a little and have found that you really have from **5am to 7pm** if you work say 8am to 5pm. With this adjustment you should be walking in the door no later that 7pm.

Several women have shared if they heard their man say *"I'm working late"* sooner or later they would become suspicious. They seemed to become less suspicious when they heard their man say *"Gotta go in early all this week!"*

Which means you should be able to leave the house around 5am; get to your "Kicker's" house and enjoy a free hour or two is cheating pleasure without your wife/ girlfriend being none the wiser!

After work is tougher, but can be done. To make this possible you will need to have an after work activity like a gym membership.

When first choosing a gym, there are rules as well..

1) Make sure your wife/ girlfriend is **NOT** a member

2) Make sure there are several kinds of this gym. (Meaning don't choose a gym where there is only one of its kind in the whole state.)

You will need to choose one with many different locations, this way even if your wife/ girlfriend decided to check up on you, go down there, and you happen to not be there, you could always say you decided to check out another location. Having a gym membership is **crucial** when cheating after work and it really can be helpful when it comes to cheating all together. Think about it, it always gives you an excuse to have an extra change of clothes at all time!

Let's say you get off of work and your "Kicker" is ready to kick. You get there, handle your business, and leave. You should immediately go straight to the gym!

First things first, hop in the shower. Now I know what you are thinking you could have showered at your "Kickers" house right…**WRONG**. You may go home smelling all right but your look is all wrong!

If you want your home team to believe that you were working out at the gym you will need gym attire and that "gym" smell. Sex sweat and gym sweat is two totally different kinds of funk.

Go to the gym, get in the gym's shower, get out, put on your gym clothes and run on the treadmill for 5 minutes (or how ever long it takes) at a high enough speed to make you have a good sweat. You will then need to make sure your t-shirt is good and soaked with sweat!

Do not towel off (turn the heat on in your car if you have to) and keep the sweat pouring until you get home. Not only will your wife/ girlfriend **NOT** want to kiss or hug you, she will not want to go any where near you until you get yourself cleaned up!

I will also advise you will need to start a gym membership before you ever start to cheat. You need to know that any new trends can be a sign that you have begun to stray so get your after work gym routine established right away.

Here's something else to note- your "Kicker" should know and understand way in advance that weekends are **OFF LIMITS!** You should only see her Monday through Friday.

When you try to see her on the weekend it's so much more difficult to try to cover up.

The whole idea of this is cheating should be easy. Between -work, meetings, and working out you are expected to be in so many places during the week this can be a piece of cake to pull it off.

Lastly, let's talk about formations, meaning sexual positions.

(NOTE: THIS LAST TOPIC IS NOT FOR THE SQUEEMISH!)

Men, let me educate you on a few things. Women are emotional, men are physical. Women want to make love, men want to fuck. Women feel emotions very differently than you. If you are walking in the mall and speak to a woman, to you- you may think it's just the courteous thing to do, to a woman- she may think you want her, thinks she's attractive, and really wants her phone number.

It can be something so small that to her means something so BIG. Having sex to you can be just you trying to get a nut, to her it can mean you love her, and want to be with her. When you decide to cheat use these sexual tips and I promise it will help to keep things simple.

MISSONARY style sex is prohibited at all times. This type of sex tells your "Kicker" that you care about her, that she means something to you, and that you could possibly be starting to fall in love with her.

Another thing, you should **NEVER** perform is **ORAL** sex on her, this too is **prohibited**! This tells her that you care enough about her to bring her oral pleasure. *Please note-Your "Kicker" performing oral sex on you should be expected.*

If she is not wet and there is no lubricant available, spit on your hand and apply it to her or use your hand/ fingers to arouse her. If none of that works spit directly on her vagina, but I repeat you performing oral sex on her will allow her to think you value her more than you truly do, and will lead to trouble.

I know this may sound harsh, but by not doing so you are letting her know she is just your side fling, never to become a member of your home team.

DOGGY style sex is recommended because it keeps you behind your "Kicker" and not underneath her. This type of sex keeps her submissive with you in control, none of that eye gazing, tongue kissing love.

By the way - speaking of kissing-**NEVER TONGUE KISS (or kiss for that matter)** a woman who you are cheating with- to many women I've spoken with (including myself) believe this act is more intimate that sex. **Do**

Not do it!! A woman will become deranged and start to believe there is a chance you may leave your wife / girlfriend for her.

RIDING- meaning letting her get on top can be allowed only to allow her to do all of the work. This method is also used to remind her of why you are cheating with her.

Your "Kicker's" job is to please you,satisfy you, and allow you to go on your hassle-free way. If you allow your "Kicker" to think that you care about her, the whole game changes. She will then begin to act differently, think differently, and start to feel differently, which will surely be all bad!

CHAPTER 5- IDENTIFING THE KICKER

Okay, now let me be perfectly honest, there are plenty of women who would not be interested in allowing you to run this whole "Kicker" methodology on them. However, there are plenty that would (this number can be increased if you play it right).

Fewer women may want to be your "Kicker" if you come out and say upon meeting them "Look I am married/ or have a woman, so I really only want you to do the things she isn't doing which is shut the hell up, satisfy me on demand, and please don't ask me for a damn thing because I can already tell you the answer will be hell-to-the-naw!"

So you will need to try a far less direct approach. Being since women are sensitive creatures they need to be able to feel that they are helping you in your situation.

Believe it or not a "Kicker" will feel special if you tell her "Baby, our sex was so good last night. You were the reason I was able to go home feeling relaxed enough to deal with my wife."

The "Kicker" wants to feel special and wants to feel they can do something for you that not even your wife/ or woman can. You will need to be 100% honest from day one with your "Kicker", she needs to know about your wife/ girlfriend/ woman/ whoever you are with. You need to tell her so that she can also assist you in your play on the field.

Many men won't tell anybody anything and the next thing you know you (the man) are cornered by the wife and the mistress. This is dangerous and silly to do especially since more women these days prefer a "married" and/ or "taken" man.

If you follow the rules of this book you can have your "Kicker" so committed to this style of cheating that even if your wife/ or woman caught you, and called to confront your "Kicker", your "Kicker" would lie so hard to cover for you that she would have you convinced!

It is very important that before you start to identify your "Kicker" that you take inventory of all of the things your wife/ or woman does that you don't like. If you hate that fact that your wife/ woman goes out to night clubs and hangs out with her friends all of the time, then you shouldn't go to a night club to find your "Kicker". If your wife / girlfriend never does her hair just pulls it back into a ponytail and that annoys you, you should go to a beauty supply store, wig shop, popular beauty salon in your town to find your "Kicker".

If your wife/ woman is loud and obnoxious, and loves to act ghetto/ignorant then you should go to an internet café, book store, popular coffee shop, or library to find your "Kicker".

The point is whatever your wife/ girlfriend is, your "Kicker" should not be. Meaning you need to seek out and find the complete opposite of what you already have. There is no point in having two of the same thing! If you have one cocky, arrogant, personality in your life why in the hell would you want another one? This will only add to your pain and frustration.

In this Chapter of Identifying the "Kicker" it is also important to tell you where **NOT** to find her. Your "Kicker" should **<u>NEVER</u>** work with you! Not only is this unethical but you will get caught guaranteed!

Another unfortunate fact is that if you are in a position of management at work and you cheat with a subordinate, you are giving your "Kicker" the power to bring forth a Sexual Harassment Lawsuit against you and your company, get you fired, or at the very least get an investigation started.

Even if your hot co-worker is coming on to you, you should **NEVER** participate! This is one "Kicker" who will end up kicking you in the end!

Actually, for the kind of position you are looking to fill you really need a "home body" type. Someone who is quiet and keeps to themselves. Someone who is not use to having a man of your caliber in her presence. Someone who will worship the very ground you walk on!

Someone who can get dressed up for you and undressed when you want them to. Someone who is comfortable just seeing you when time permits. Now I am not saying that your "Kicker" has to be unattractive with low self esteem, no I'm not saying that at all!

From my conversations with women while writing this book, I found many of the women who would be considered "attractive" by society's standard were **more** willing to be the "Kicker" than the women who were considered by society's standard as unattractive and/or overweight.

During my talks with some of the "more attractive women" I spoke with, many admitted that they had been physically and mentally scarred by the abuse they received. This treatment made them less interested in the physical/ financial attributes of the man and more interested in the treatment from the man.

Several of these women felt the men they had been with were intimidated because of their beauty, and because of this treated them badly. Often times they said they were lied to, abused, deceived, mistreated, and cheated on.

So because of this, many admitted that they would be more agreeable to being a "Kicker". One simply put it "I would rather be cheated with than cheated on". She went on to share she would definitely be open to this if the man would just be up front in the beginning, so she would know what or who she was dealing with!

Many of the "less attractive women" (based on society's standard) admitted they deserved more, and that they needed more. It would appear they demanded more as well, one even shared, "I may be overweight, but I am pretty as hell and a man needs to recognize!"

More than half of these women shared even if a man was honest and up front about wanting to cheat on their wife/ girlfriend with them they would decline. One woman shared her reason for declining stating "I don't eat half a burger, and I don't want half a man!" (Meaning she wants "all or nothing" as she put it!)

The point in me sharing all of this is you don't have to choose a "Kicker" who is so repulsive that you have to insist that she place black curtains over her blinds just to block out the sunlight so it seems dark outside all day long.

When identifying your "Kicker" use this check list because she will need to meet these minimum qualifications....

1) She must have her own place (as previously stated)

2) She must have her own car- She needs to be mobile at all times

3) She must have a job- a woman who is not working will be looking for a different kind of man and relationship, this one will not work for her as she will always be asking for or needing something

4) She must be single- she needs to be available to you on *your* time and being since you will never be able to have a set schedule, her having a man will only confuse things.

Identifying your "Kicker" will take sometime and effort. This is not something that can be identified after only meeting once or twice. You will need to invest plenty of hours conversing, role playing, and interviewing. It is also recommended that when you are speaking with your potential "Kicker" that you tell her why you are searching for a "Kicker" in the first place.

Many women have shared with me they will ask a man what his type is only because they had the intention on becoming that "type."

They would also encourage the man to share what he disliked about their mate or past mates, because they had every intention of being the opposite of this so it would be that much easier to get him and keep him interested.

You will need to lay it out for your potential "Kicker" by letting her know what things disturb you about your mate currently. This way she will know if these were the kinds of traits you were looking for you could just go home.

You will also need to spend a great deal of time carefully listening to her. If when referring to her past relationships or her likes and dislikes she shares things like...

- Her last man use to wine and dine her and buy her things
- Her last man would do things like pay her rent and/ or take her to expensive places and trips
- Her last man still calls her/ or they are still close friends
- She has a lot of female friends
- She likes to do things like go out the clubs/ parties

Discontinue all contact immediately; this is not a potential "Kicker" for you.

You should be listening for things like...

- I love to stay home and watch movies
- I really don't have a lot of female friends

- I don't need a man to take care of me; I take care of myself
- My last man cheated on me

Many of the women who provided feedback shared **they would prefer to be cheated with, than cheated on.**

One of the women I surveyed shared why- "It's simple, when I found out my man was cheating on me I felt like a victim, powerless, like everyone knew what was going on except me!" "At least by being cheated with, I am in the know, this way I am in control!"

So with that being said listening for some of these key phrases will assist you in screening out some of the women who will cause problems- almost right off the bat! You really have to think about it like this, this is a job and you are the hiring manager! Sure you may have to interview and decline several candidates, however in doing so this will pay off. By asking the right questions, and take a mental note, you should be able to fill your "Kicker" position in no time!

CHAPTER 6- HOW TO KEEP YOUR KICKER ONLY WANTING TO KICK

If you think about Professional Football never has a Kicker been selected #1 in the first round of the draft. Never is the Kicker the star player on the team, and never is the Kicker the highest paid player in the league or on the team.

So what is it that keeps the Kicker wanting to kick? I would like to think the reason is they enjoy what they do and they are good at it! If they should happen to be a Kicker for a winning team that just makes the job that much sweeter!

When searching for a "Kicker" you must find one who enjoys what they do. If they enjoy the job and like the team, they will want to keep doing the job for the team and will do it to the best of their ability! This is the very reason your "Kicker" must immediately know that she is kicking for a winning team.

You know that saying "Image is everything" well it is! You must build an image with your "Kicker" that let's her know you are the **shit!!** You have to walk like you are the best man she could ever get. Talk to her as if you are the best man she could ever get, and believe that you are the best man she **will** ever get! If you want her to believe this you must first believe it yourself!

If you followed the tips and rules in the last Chapter in selecting your "Kicker" she will worship your very essence. If you present yourself as if you are the biggest thing to ever happen to her; she will believe it as well!

Also let's think back to Chapter 3. One of the Rules was to never give your "Kicker" money, however just because you are not giving or spending money on your "Kicker" that does not mean you should not be spending an adequate amount of time with her.

Spending time does not always have to be physical time spent; it could be a call on the way home from work or during the day. (When doing this please refer to the call tip guide in Chapter 3 and Chapter 7). It could also be a quick stop to say hello.

This however does **not** include text messages and/or emails. This gets you men caught time and time again. Not to mention leaves a paper trail that will lead in no other direction than yours!

You should also have a habit of keeping your word. If you say you are going to come over then do so, if you say you are going to call, call. Your "Kicker" will never truly be there for you if she can not count on you.

You also need to make sure that when you are with your "Kicker", she feels she is a very important woman to you. Although it is not necessary to ever tell her that you love her.

Telling your "Kicker" that you love her will change the flow of the game. You know that saying "If you tell a lie long enough you may start to believe it!" Well you for damn sure don't want to run that risk and definitely not the risk of your "Kicker" believing it!

To keep your "Kicker" only wanting to kick you have to convince her that she has the best job and most importantly that she does the best job.

You need to consistently let her know that you missed her, that you need her sexually, that she can make you feel a way that not even your wife/ girlfriend can. Tell her you want her, can't keep your mind off her, and that she is the best sexually you've ever been with.

Even if she's not, tell her anyway! By doing so you will make her feel so special that she won't mind pleasing you to the best of her ability anytime you choose. (You really shouldn't have to outright tell a complete lie about her being the best sexually- if she is not the best she should be damn close, because if not what's the point of you kicking it with her).

You also have to be willing to "dick" her down from time to time; every now and again you will have to put a little extra effort into it. This **DOES NOT** mean performing sex outside of the sexual guidelines. It does mean that you take an afternoon off work and spend it with her; lay with her a little longer than usual after having sex, and/ or making the sex last longer than usual to satisfy her. (I would think you would already know how to do this, but for those who don't know this means jacking off prior).

Remember there are plenty of women who will cheat with a man for years, but if the sex is good they may cheat forever, and will have no problem doing so!

Men also seem to forget the power of words. They say "actions are stronger than words," but I can't tell! Words can make a woman feel in such a way that if you repeatedly tell them you love them but repeatedly show them **you don't**, they will believe your words over your actions!

Women will stay in abusive relationships with their abusers for years as long as the man tells her he loves her. Many women will make up excuses for the man's actions and stay with him simply based on his words.

The problem is you men take words too far. You don't need to say "I love you" instead you need to say things like "You have some of the most beautiful eyes I have ever seen" or "I love the way you make me feel when you put your mouth on me" "You are my most favorite girl, you know that?"

If you use these words correctly your "Kicker" will melt like butter guaranteed. If you are complimenting her mouth, look her directly in her eyes, take your finger and lightly trace the outline of her lips. Or if you are complimenting her eyes, again look her directly in the eyes and gently run the back of your hand down the side of her face.

Another compliment that seems to give a woman chills is to compliment the curve down the center of her back.

As she is facing you look her in the eyes, hug her and run your hands down the center curve of her bare back while saying, "This is one of the sexiest part of your body, damn you are so sexy!" Don't be surprised if your "Kicker" falls to the ground and starts performing oral sex on you right at that very minute.

Following your words up with subtle actions will have your "Kicker" reliving each minute you spend with her over and over again.

So the complete recipe for keeping your "Kicker" only wanting to kick is…..

Keeping your word (if you are not sure that you can come over don't say you will be there) **+ A little extra sexual effort on your behalf on occasion + plenty of compliments = a very satisfied Kicker!**

SCORE

CHAPTER 7- PREVENTING THE PERSONAL FOUL

In the game of football, often the Quarterback will start to get in his rhythm, and his plays will start coming together. Once they do his team will start to gain yardage. The next thing that could happen is he has thrown the perfect spiral pass and after he has thrown the ball out of no where he gets **HIT!** If the ref doesn't see it or even if it is challenged and over ruled, whatever yardage that was gained is now lost!

The very same thing could happen in this situation. In this game you can go from gaining yardage to losing the ball, or even being sacked very quickly!

We've discussed how to identify and interact with your "Kicker", now we must discuss your home team and how you treat them.

Most wives/ girlfriends that have been with their man for any length of time will know their habits, likes, and dislikes. If you all of a sudden start to like asparagus when you absolutely hated it before your wife/ girlfriend will notice. If after 5 years of marriage you have never asked your woman to lick whip cream off of your nipples, the day you do, she will notice.

Points being if there is anything you haven't done in the past with your wife/girlfriend that you have been doing with your "Kicker"- **don't start!** This is a red flag that something is going on and she may start to investigate!

I also would like you to get in the habit of preventive maintenance! This is preventing possible problems before they arise.

Let's discuss the dangers of **CELL PHONES….**

Many men these days will lock their cell phones and the phone will then require a numeric code to unlock it. Your wife/girlfriend will probably know all of your four digit codes (like your birthday month/day, full birth year i.e. 1981) they may even know your social security number, bank code, etc.

The point is even if they can not crack the code they will at least have enough information to get online (which is the way most cellular phone companies allow you to access your bill) and get every phone number you have called, time, date, and length of the call.

A wife recently shared with me that one night she just decided to look through her husband's phone while he was in the shower. She said she didn't get too far because his phone was locked. Later that evening she logged onto his cell phone provider's website and attempted to gain access that way, but she needed the password.

She logged under the "forgot password" tab, entered in enough of his information like her husband's date of birth, social security number, name of his high school, favorite sports team's name, and PRESTO CHANGE-O. The next thing she knew she was online writing down numbers that were incoming or outgoing that appeared on his bill multiple times.

Long story short, the next thing I know she was calling me asking when this book was going to be available for purchase. She said she was going to purchase a copy of this book for her husband, wrap it up with a big red bow, insert the divorce papers she had filed and give it to his ass for Christmas!

Come to find out her husband had been cheating with his secretary. How was she able to confirm it?? Simple, she called the number from his cell phone, and the woman answered "Hi baby I missed you!" The wife confronted the woman on the other end, and after the wife ranted and promised, "Bitch

I'll kick your ass, I know where you work!"
(even though she didn't) The secretary
became so frightened she confessed and told
everything!

(I will get to online billing in a minute)

You need to get in the habit of not using
commonly known dates and bank codes or
parts of your social security number as your
cell phone codes.

You will also need to get in the habit of
deleting each incoming and outgoing call
from or to your "Kicker" as soon as the call
is done. Under no circumstance should you
ever delete the whole call log. By doing so it
will be very obvious you are trying to hide
something.

As previously mentioned you will need to do
away with text messaging, not only is there a
possibility these may be found, but this is the
one piece of evidence that can never be

erased or deleted. These messages can be saved forever and even forwarded.

SPEAKING OF MESSAGING…THIS WOULD INCLUDE VOICEMAIL!

You will need to tell your "Kicker" to never leave you a message period! Too many men get caught by the wife/girlfriend retrieving a hot and steamy message that some woman has left. To ensure this never happens to you I suggest in addition to telling your "Kicker" to never leave you a message, you take it a step further.

You will need to call yourself so many times that your voice mail can no longer accept any new messages. Every five days or so you will need to call yourself and record new messages so that your voice mail box always says it's full! (if possible do not even set up your voice mail system or have it removed)

More rules??- *I know, I'm sorry, but you men need them...* ☺

RULE- NEVER EVER ACCEPT CELL PHONE CAMERA PHOTOS! MONITOR CELL PHONE CALLS AT ALL TIMES, AND STORE YOUR KICKER'S PHONE NUMBER UNDER A NAME THAT NO ONE WOULD EVER SUSPECT

I've heard so many women say they found out their man had been cheating by tapping into either their man's cell phone bill or the cell phone itself.

Men are visual beings, and it would make perfect sense that you would enjoy receiving an intimate picture from your "Kicker" right? **WRONG!**

Do **NOT** accept any camera pictures from your "Kicker" for any reason! Who's to say your woman won't go through your phone or simply need to use your phone? When she finds that picture (and believe me she will) before you can even get a word in you'll be dodging flying objects trying to convince your woman she did not see what she saw!

Now let's talk about the phone bill itself. Most bills are either mailed to your home address or either available to view online. Online anything is all bad. A woman can hack into an online account faster than she can change her toe nail polish!

And while I am on the topic of "online", let me discuss social networking websites. Here again **<u>anything online</u>** is a **BIG "NO-NO"!** Do not connect with, or contact your "Kicker" online. This will lead to a trail that leads right back to you. Remember anything that someone can read, print out, refer back to, copy, or paste- **DON'T DO IT!**

Now regarding your online phone bill please discontinue your online cell phone account immediately! Ask your phone company for a paper bill. In doing so you will need to let them know that you have a different mailing address.

You will need to use a P.O. Box that no one knows you have but you!

The natural choice for many of you prior to reading this book may have been to using a friend's address. However if you ever fall out with this friend you run the risk of this friend telling your woman that you have been using their address and/ or they could take it upon themselves to take the bill over to her. Not to mention having to worry about the "what ifs" are enough to trip you up and make you sloppy.

Have you ever heard the term "I do my dirt all by myself"? Well this phrase absolutely applies...the less people know about your "Kicker" the better. Even if you thought to use your work address this is all bad as well. What if you get fired or let go, most companies will forward your mail back to your house. Look, I never said cheating is "free" but due to the fact that you will not be spending money on your "Kicker", this should be an investment you are willing to make!

The last part of this rule is to properly store your Kicker's telephone number in your cell phone.

Most of the time men think they should not store the name and number, but if a woman sees a number popping up multiple times on multiple days with no name attached this sends up a red flag. It is far less suspicious to see a name and phone number appear especially if it's a name she is comfortable with.

Please do not read this and think "I know I will store my "Kicker's" name and number under my mother's name"! No dice, your wife/ girlfriend should know this number, if she doesn't she may get a bright idea to one day call your mother and introduce herself if she doesn't already know her, or even call to plan a surprise party/ gathering for you. The minute she dials this number and your mother does not answer- you are screwed- and not the way you would've hoped!

You should do the unthinkable. Store your "Kicker's" number under your boss or manager's name and number! Think about it…this way your boss/ manager's name and number can appear anytime day or night and your woman would be non the wiser!

Please follow steps 1 through 4

Step 1- Program your boss/ manager's name in the address book in your cell phone

Step 2- Enter your work office phone number in the work field

Step 3- Enter your boss/ manager's mobile number in the mobile field

Step 4- Enter your "Kicker's" number in the home phone number field.

HOWEVER -THERE IS ONE HUGE EXCEPTION TO SAVING YOUR KICKER'S NAME AND PHONE NUMBER AS YOUR BOSS/ MANAGER

If your boss/ manager is a hot, sexy, female, this will not work, as I am sure you can figure out why.

If this does end up being the case, do the absolute unthinkable…save your "Kicker's" name and number under your childhood Pastor's name. (Oh don't go gettin' all spiritual now- you are cheating remember) I don't care if you haven't been to church since the year of the rat, save it anyway! Be sure to randomly mention to your wife/ girlfriend you ran into your childhood Pastor, who you exchanged numbers with because he wanted to be able to call from time to time to touch bases, possibly even pray with you. Now I can tell some of you are a little shaky on whether you can pull this off, so let's role play…

Say you missed a call at 1am, (which your "Kicker" should know better) the next day your woman asks who was that who called; your natural response should be "Oh, yeah that was my Pastor I was telling you about. I called him back today and he said he was moved by the spirit and wanted to lead me in prayer for faith and marriage!"

Now she may not completely go for it, but she won't go too far in disbelieving you, because after all who would lie about such a thing!

Now if you can tell she is in complete disbelief take it a step further and say "Man, when I was a kid he used to call our house at all times of the day and night which is apart of the reason we stopped attending his church!"

Now in extreme cases she may ask to speak with your Pastor. (Which means you should have purchased this book much sooner because you must have been slippin' up for some time now) If she does simply tell her that he is leaving town to Africa and is doing some world ministering and won't be back for some time, but when he does you would love for her to meet him!

Now if you are following this book the case of your "Kicker" calling at 1am will never happen. Let's not forget the earlier lesson of **"ON PEAK VS. OFF PEAK"**, your "Kicker" should be following this to the letter but in the event she slips up, I always want you to have a back up plan.

Anyway just be sure your "Kicker" is saved as one of the two.

But wait…not so fast…since we are on the topic of phone number storage, if you ever have to call your "Kicker" from another number besides your cell phone, say for example you have to call her from work because your cell phone is dying or is dead, **ALWAYS BE SURE TO BLOCK THE NUMBER!!** Women in general are very resourceful and will save any number you have ever called them from.

You never want to be able to give your "Kicker" an alternative way to contact you, by doing so it will lead to trouble and it will make it more difficult to cut her off if you ever need to!

Ok, I believe you got that point, let's discuss another part of preventing the personal foul.

One of the biggest tell-tale signs you are cheating is your lack of interest in sex. If you use to want to have sex multiple times of day with your wife/ girlfriend and now all of a sudden you go straight to bed without even so much as a good-night kiss, this will confirm sooner or later there is trouble in paradise!

I don't care if you use to have to pout and argue with your wife/ girlfriend because of her lack of sexual appetite, your lack of sex will tell your wife/ girlfriend that you are getting it elsewhere, which will lead her to unleash a full investigation!

Another tell- tale sign will be when your solider won't stand at attention, as to say. On very rare occasions this can happen when you begin to feel guilty or have a hard time separating the two.

You lay there thinking, "Man I keeping having thoughts of the sex I had with my "Kicker" or "Damn I have to stay focused, what if I slip up and say my "Kicker's" name out loud"

You need to get in the habit of being okay with what you are doing. If you are feeling guilty about being with your "Kicker"- **STOP!** If thinking about your "Kicker" makes you hard at an instance, when it comes to sleeping with your wife/ or woman, envision your wife/ girlfriend is really your "Kicker".

Also get in the habit of having sex without saying specific names; you should only be using terms like honey, baby, and babe. This way even if in the heat of the moment you slip, you'll slip and say a term that will be accepted by your wife/ girlfriend!

CHAPTER 8- AVOIDING THE BLITZ

Okay let's quickly explain the term "blitz". As I understand in football this happens when the defense can't cover all of the offensive players, so the quarterback is pressured. When a blitz is done correctly the quarterback is sacked, thrown off his timing, or forced to throw an interception.

Here you are, you are relaxed and feeling good. Everybody is happy. Your team is happy, your "Kicker" is happy, and most importantly you are happy! Then all of a sudden you start to feel a little pressure.

What normally happens in life is when one thing starts to go south- everything does! I am not sure in which order things will start to unravel but sooner or later it will. It's how you handle the situation that will hold off the pressure, or consume you.

The key to avoiding the "cheating" blitz is to switch things up with your "Kicker". You should never establish a routine with your "Kicker". You should not be doing the same thing, on the same day, at the same time with her.

If last Monday you hung out with your "Kicker", the following Monday you should come home early and surprise your wife/ girlfriend with flowers, candy, night on the town, etc.

Look, let's be real. On certain days you should know it will be virtually impossible to please all parties. So you need to be prepared to do a quarterback sneak if you have to!

To assist you with this- here are a few sample pressures and how you should handle them…

Pressure from your wife/ girlfriend to spend more time with her- they always want the finer things in life, but they are the first to complain when you start working longer hours.

What should you do...?

Simply begin to spend more time with her, however far less money on her. Say things like "I wanted to take you to that one expensive restaurant, but since I haven't been working long hours things are a little tight, but it's cool just to hang out in the house- isn't it?"

After about a week of this she will be waking your ass up extra early to get you out of the door for work on time!

Pressure from your wife/ girlfriend about how many hours you spend in the gym- (here again she will want you to look good, but she won't understand why it's necessary to be committed in the gym.)

What should you do...?

Skip the gym for a couple of days, and start to poke your stomach out. Tell her how obesity runs in your family and ask her "If I gained 100 pounds you'd still love me right?"

Even if you are already out of shape do this anyway. If she was never into your looks, physique, then this may not work. But your newly found interest to be active, and stay healthy should buy you some understanding.

Now it's not uncommon for your wife/girlfriend to want to join a gym as well. Encourage her to do so. Let her know that joining the same gym would be a huge distraction and she should look into a "women's" fitness center.

Another good suggestion is to tell her you want to have a "get fit" challenge and by joining different gyms it will make the competition more exciting. Being since you will not be working out together you will not be able to see the actual workout and progress each other are making. Even go as far as to select a start and stop date, prizes for the winner, etc.

Let's just say your mate is hardcore, not going for it at all, grab her around the waist, pull her close, look her in the eyes and say, "Baby the thought of you working up a sweat, squatting, bending over, picking up weights is making me hard already. Neither of us will ever get anything done!"

Pressure from your "Kicker" to spend more time with her-

I would like to hope that you have a "Kicker" who is just happy to come in when needed and Kick, but even they can start to become too comfortable. One minute they were all too happy to please you, and the next minute they start asking/ expecting for a little more time.

What should you do…? Spend less time with her. Don't make up excuses as to why you are less available, tell her the truth.

Telling the truth to your "Kicker" will get you much further - trust me!

Let her know that you are starting to have serious doubts as to whether she can handle the situation anymore. Remind her that she knew what it was in the very beginning, tell her you want her to think about things and you will call her in a week.

If she calls you, don't answer! If she immediately says "No, I mean I was just asking, but it's fine I understand you have your woman/ wife/ family, **DO IT ANYWAY!!** You will need to punish her for even asking! It's like putting a kid in time out. If you take away from her what she has, she will appreciate it when she gets it back, and will never again complain about it!

There are women who will participate in this for years, because the thought of not having you at all frightens them so badly, that they will not only put up with it, they'll love it!

I could go on and about pressures from a "Kicker", but what for? You need to know and understand that your "Kicker" should be treated in such a manner they know what time it is!

The thought of you having an unruly wife/ girlfriend and "Kicker" is insane. Your "Kicker" **does not** call the shots, and they should never tell you what to do. In the very beginning you need to establish you are the quarterback. This is your team, this is your show!

Little things turn into big things very quickly if you are not careful. Little comments from your "Kicker" like "Where have you been?" or "I thought you were coming over hours ago!" lead to trouble **FAST**. You need to nip all those kinds of comments in the bud.

Anytime she says something like that…..**LEAVE**. Turn right around and walk out the door, although not before telling her.

"Look if I wanted to be nagged or hassled I could have just gone straight home!"

Before you are able to hit the driveway good, don't be surprised if she's already apologizing, but that's not enough! She will need to feel the burn and sting of seeing you drive off, and the stress of not knowing when or if she will see you again.

Expect her to then call or text you. Say **NOTHING!** Do not answer or text back, instead go to the gym and work out. By the time you get done with an hour work out she will have called so many times that your cell phone battery will begin to blink and signal it's about to die. Your "Kicker" at this point will be at her house by this time snottin', and crying, wanting to kick her own ass for opening her big mouth in the first place!

Now in the event she is one of those women who are a little tougher to crack, if she doesn't call **don't call her**! The first person to call- **LOSES**, do what ever you have to but under no circumstance should you make that call. Just be patient she will call, sooner or later she will!

After about a full week has passed she will have felt the burn and sting of not being able to kick it with you on your terms. You can rest assure she will not take this approach with you anytime soon, and instead will go out of her way to prove to you she is perfectly fine with the situation-just the way it is!

CHAPTER 9- SACKING THE QUARTERBACK

I really hate to have to include this chapter, however being since nothing is fool proof (not even this guide- although it's pretty damn close) I find it necessary to include it just in case I need to bail you out of trouble!

In the game of football a sack is when the defensive line/player rushes through and knocks the quarterback to the ground while he still has possession of the ball.

So being since I have established you are the quarterback, trying to make forward progress down the field to make a touchdown, the unthinkable has happened, you have just been sacked.

Scenario #1

That inquisitive mate of yours has gone through your phone and started calling back phone numbers of people she doesn't recognize. She comes across a phone number which is saved in your phone as your boss "Mr. Johnson- CEO", however when she dials the number a female on the other end answers "Hey baby"

Your mate becomes irate, starts asking all kinds of questions, and then calls you into the room.

Should you...

A) Snatch the phone out of your girlfriend/ wife's hand and hang the phone up

B) Start cursing out your girlfriend/ wife for being so damn nosey

C) Tell the woman on the other end of the phone to tell your wife/girlfriend that nothing ever happened

D) All of the above

E) None of the above

If you answered "**A**" it's a good thing you purchased this guide! I know, I know it seems like the right thing to do, and you will probably be wrapped up in the heat of the moment, however stay calm!!!

The correct answer is "E"- none of the above" You should do nothing! Your "Kicker" should know what to do. They should know to play dumb, act as though they don't know the number and that they acted in haste. Your "Kicker" should know to say she only glanced at the phone number and that her and her husband accidentally traded cell phones because they both have the same phone. Your "Kicker" should say she accidentally took her husband's phone and that her husband took hers by mistake.

She should know to say her phone number is only a digit or two off from the number showing on the caller i.d., so she assumed it was her husband calling from her cell phone because the numbers were so similar. Now if your wife/ girlfriend are really sharp she might ask, "If that's the case why wouldn't your husband have your name and number saved in his phone?"

This is when your "Kicker" should know to say "Oh, I actually just got a new phone number which is why he hasn't saved it yet, and also why I assumed it was him calling when I saw your phone number!"

If further questioned she should know the name she is saved under, and should know to recite the name to prove that's "Mr. Johnson" is her husband. If further probed after that your "Kicker" should know to hang up!

It is important to note because you have saved your "Kicker's" number under your boss/ pastor/ etc name this little lie should work like a breeze. You and your "Kicker" should also role play, read this book, and practice these scenarios together so that neither you nor she will ever be caught off guard!

(Now if your wife/girlfriend is the extra crazy, "now I'm about to call your job tomorrow and talk to your boss" type. You may need to skip the whole storage technique, and just memorize your "Kicker's" number and be sure to dial and delete after every call)

Ok, now let's try another one...

Scenario #2

You and your wife/ girlfriend are having a wonderful evening out on the town. You have taken her to her favorite restaurant and she is a little tipsy. You are just about to leave the restaurant when you look over and notice your "Kicker" having dinner with an older woman who appears to be your "Kicker's" mother.

Your wife/ girlfriend sees what you are looking at and says the older woman is "Mrs. So and So"(her old teacher from High School). She then proceeds to tell you that she wants to go over and say "hi"!

Should you...

A) Fake an asthma attack and say you have to leave immediately as you have forgotten your inhaler in the car

B) Tell her that you have been waiting to rip her clothes off all night and she needs to go wait in the car and unloosen her bra to get ready for you while you pay

C) Tell her that she is really drunk and she wouldn't want her childhood teacher to tell everyone she saw her that way

D) Get mad and tell her "That's your damn problem, you are always focusing on everybody else but me with yo' social butterfly ass, that's why I'm cheating on you!"

The correct answer is "**C**". Play on the fact that she has been drinking. Nobody wants an elder or old teacher to see them all drunk and belligerent. Remember we don't want any type of connection between your wife/ girlfriend and your "Kicker".

For all we know you could fall out with your "Kicker" and she could ask her mom, about your wife/ girlfriend. Who knows if the mom would be able to dig up enough information to find your wife/ girlfriend's old address, or much worse your wife/ girlfriend's parents' address?

You need to avoid all possible risk at all times. You also need to be the man in ALL relationships, meaning what you say goes! Not saying you have to be an ass about it, however your team needs to know your suggestions should be followed.

If you have not reached this point with your wife/ girlfriend you should not be out anywhere with her until you have.

If any of these above listed scenarios are not played correctly…game over…you will be sacked! This is something you simply can **not** afford to happen. I mean hooking up with the "Kicker" is cool and all but she is not worth losing your whole team for.

Alright last one guys…lets try to get this one right.

Scenario #3

Your "Kicker" has been acting up for awhile and it's time to cut her off. You call her and tell her it's over. Before you can hang up, she tells you she has followed you home and knows exactly where you live. She then tells you she is going to go to your house and tell your wife/ girlfriend everything.

Should you...

A) Tell her you don't want to end it and that you are willing to work it out if she doesn't tell

B) Invite her to a local night club and when she gets there have some of your old female friends beat the hell out of her

C) Go home and forewarn your wife/ girlfriend by telling her everything

D) Tell her to go right ahead. Let her know that your wife/ girlfriend knows everything already which is the reason why you have to end it. Also let her know that your wife/ girlfriend has been boxing professionally for years and wants to see her so she can A-town stomp your "Kicker's" ass all up and down the block. Then tell her after she gets run down by your wife/ girlfriend like a lion on a gazelle you will be sure to call the cops and have her taken to jail for trespassing.

The correct answer is "**D**". If I know anything its most women are scary, sure they may "talk a good game" but when it comes to fist to face action they normally want no parts of that. Not to mention one of the worse beat downs I ever saw was a woman beating the hell out of another woman for sleeping with her husband.

Not to mention by calling her bluff, you forever take the power away from her threatening you anytime she wants.

But let's just say your "Kicker" is the one variable I didn't consider…what if she says "O.K", and the next thing you know…

DING DONG…THIS CRAZY BITCH IS AT YOUR FRONT DOOR….

special note- there are women in general who will try to follow you to your home/ job. Always be on the look out and take alternative routes to ensure this does not happen to you. Remember your "Kicker" should NOT know where you work or live

CHAPTER 10- CHALLENGING THE CALL

ATTENTION ALL MEN IN THIS (or in a similar) SCENARIO- You better get that red challenge flag ready because your "Kicker" is really at your front door.

Or you as the Quarterbacks- may wanna call a time out for this one...

In almost any sport I can recall, whenever a foul is called the offending player always shakes his head furiously as to say "What?" "Who me, no I didn't commit a pentality!" "What, I didn't bit any ear!" "Hell naw, I didn't forearm that player who's now on the ground, rolling around in agony and pain!"

And without fail the minute it is determined they are guilt of the charge, they throw a fit! Cursing, yelling, and sometimes getting ejected all while still claiming it wasn't them.

Even all the way to the bench or locker room, they still deny the charge. Even when the referee has reviewed the play, they still swear they didn't do it.

Have you ever wondered why they do this? They do this because sometimes they get away with it. Sometimes the charge is over ruled and they continue to play as if nothing ever happened.

O.k., play ball....

Your "Kicker" is at your door. Three things are extremely important here...

1) **STAY CALM**

2) It is your job to calmly get your "Kicker" away from your door as fast as possible

3) **DENY, DENY, DENY!**

I don't care if your "Kicker" has you on tape (which should never happen) deny it anyway.

Always say things like, "She is crazy!", "I don't know her!", "I didn't do it!", and "It wasn't me!"

It is your job to make your "Kicker" seem unstable, crazy, and flat out insane. Now this shouldn't be that hard to do, I mean after all she did just tell you she had been following you to your house, and actually showed up!

Now at this point your wife/ girlfriend will be **VERY** angry however your job is to make her angry at your "Kicker" not at you!

In no way should you allow your wife/ girlfriend to physically hit or strike your "Kicker" and **definitely do not allow your "Kicker" to even think about physically touching your wife/ girlfriend.** Not only will allowing this to happen cost you and your team financially (maybe even jail time), but this could also end up in court which would provide a controlled environment for your "Kicker" to better present her case against you!

You will however need to become very foul in language towards your "Kicker". You will need to attack her appearance, use vulgar language, call her out of her name repeatedly, profess your undying love and respect for your wife/girlfriend, and flat out call your "Kicker" a "liar" to her face.

Please do not participate in going back and forth with your "Kicker", instead calmly pull your wife/ girlfriend into the house and close the door. I would hate for you to have to call the police because again this would only allow your "Kicker" to be able to present her case against you, but in extreme cases you just might have to.

Since your "Kicker" has done the unthinkable you will need to do the following immediately...

1) Change your cell phone number (now your wife/ girlfriend may wonder why

this is necessary since this crazy chick according to you never had your cell phone number, but explain to her for weeks you'd been receiving hang up calls or someone breathing on the phone).

2) Get an order of protection against your "stalker" formerly known as your "Kicker".
3) Under no circumstance should you ever see or speak to your "Stalker" again
4) Immediately begin damage control with your wife/ girlfriend.

I know what you're thinking "but earlier in the guide you said the easiest way is the best way, so why wouldn't I just confess?"

If you do you might as well kiss what little bit of sanity you have goodbye!!

From the moment you confess, it won't ever stop (remember women are emotional creatures). Your wife/ girlfriend will want to know times, places, what, when, how. Did you have sex with her? Was it good? How many times? Positions? Is she better than me? Do you love her? Why? Were you attracted to her? Did she love you? How long has this been going on? Where is she from? What's her sign? Can she cook? I wanna talk to her, etc.

You will be answering her questions and reliving this ***every single day for the rest of your life with her.***

It's also good to know if you do confess and if she is one of the very few women (and I do mean very few) who does leave you- if you were married and had a little bit of money, you may now kiss that goodbye.

I will say for the most part wives/ girlfriends will not leave they will stay around with one sole purpose in mind and that will be to make your life ***miserable!***

So here's the alternative…confess and she will probably stay, and just bring it up everyday **versus** not confess, she will still bring it up on occasion, but because you never gave her any hard facts she will eventually get over it and stop mentioning it all together.

I had a woman tell me she had every intention on getting past her man's cheating after he confessed, however every time they had a simple argument or disagreement the thought of his cheating always came rushing back.

Another woman shared with me she got off of work early and stopped by to surprise her boyfriend of 5 years. She said she pulled up to his condo, but couldn't tell if he was home because he normally parked in the garage.

She said her first mind told her to park, get out, and try the front door handle, so she did. To her surprise the front door opened.

She walked in, headed straight into his

bedroom and sitting on the bed (she had just had sex in the day before) was her boyfriend and some woman, however to this day he still denies this happened.

Now he couldn't deny the woman was there, but he could (and still does) deny anything ever happened meaning sexually. The women said she was so shocked at the time she just turned around and ran out of the house. By the time she came back to her senses and went back to the house to confront him, the woman was gone!

The trust was broken between them, however she stayed. She stayed because he denied he was ever with the woman she saw. He told her that he barely knew her, and in doing so this helped him to have to answer any personal questions about her. Any personal questions she asked him, he just kept saying "I told you, I don't know her like that!" So because he would not give up any real information, his girlfriend said she never knew for sure one way or the other if he was telling the truth.

Even when she would become angry and bring it up, he just kept to his original story that he barely knew her, and that he had never been with her. With no real proof, this woman said she had to eventually let it go!

Now there may be some cases where proof is actually presented. Let's say your "Kicker" somehow met up with your wife/girlfriend. If you followed this guide at the very most, the only thing she (your "Kicker") should have are her cell phone or cell records to show your wife/ girlfriend.

Yes, that would be enough for your wife/girlfriend to assume something was going on. So in this case you should confirm you had been "talking" to her on a friendship level because she (your "Kicker") had been having relationship issues, but that's all. The key word here is "confirm". Always have the charges laid out against you **first** before you "confirm" anything. You need to find out what all your wife/ girlfriend has been told before you say anything.

Anything you admit to (even if you admit to only exchanging phone numbers) please expect to receive a long list of additional questions but still stick to your original claim "Nothing ever happened!" **Only** admit to what you absolutely have to, but never admit to the act itself!

Here again, I don't care if your wife/ girlfriend saw video footage of you butt naked, in a pair of black ankle socks, with your initials engraved on them – challenge the call- anyway…

DENY, DENY, DENY!!!

CHAPTER 11- RUNNING INTO THE KICKER

In the game of professional football, anytime there is incidental contact with the kicker after the ball has been kicked you can expect to receive a 5 yard penalty. This is not to be confused with "roughing the kicker" which in the game of football (as in real life) would carry a more severe penalty.

Let me be the first to say, if you should so happen to see your ex "Kicker" your first thought might be to "rough the kicker", but for what? This is extra drama that can easily be avoided, and so too can running into the Kicker.

I recommend you avoid any and all places or neighborhoods your "Kicker" might be in. You should also avoid returning back to the place you met her. Most women will return to the place they originally met you in hopes of running back into you.

Being since you should have (by now) changed your phone number, got a restraining order, and never provided any alternative ways for her to contact you- you should be fine.

It should be smooth sailing, but I still want to plan for the worse and hope for the best, so... just in case you do run into her, stick to the following and do not deviate one tiny bit...

1) Stay **CALM**
2) Do not make a scene
3) Do not allow her to make a scene
4) Do not engage in small talk
5) Do not debate the facts
6) Do not ask her why
7) Do not allow her to explain
8) Do not stay- leave immediately
9) And definitely **DO NOT** give her your new cell phone number.

Your interaction with her is over and you can not afford to make the same mistake twice! Even if she persist and wants to engage in an argument or conversation- **don't**- just be the bigger man, walk away, and keep walking.

I wanted to be sure to include this Chapter because I wanted you be a ready for whatever.

Being caught off guard is another sure fire way to trouble. Not to mention because you are denying (still) to your wife/ girlfriend that anything ever happened, and trying to get back in your wife's/ girlfriend's good graces, you really don't need any distractions.

CHAPTER 12- ENJOYING HOME FIELD ADVANTAGE AND OTHER LAST MINUTE TIPS…

In sports including the game of football, teams will strive for home field advantage. The reason this is so widely sought after is you get to play on and are familiar with your own turf, your own field, and in front of your own crowd. While in these types of scenarios players tend to be more relaxed, less jittery, more supported, and prepared.

This guide is **YOUR HOME FIELD ADVANTAGE!**

By the time you consider cheating to be an option; you will need to make sure you have read this book from cover to cover several times. Remember to be able to pull this off it will take skill, knowledge, and determination. It's probably not a good idea to let your wife/ girlfriend know you have purchased this book either. If they should so happen to mention this book play dumb and say something like "No babe, I have never heard of the book but it sounds dumb as hell to me!"

I began this book by congratulating you on purchasing this book, now I congratulate you on cheating by this book. You started as the Quarterback of your team and it was my job to make you into the **STAR** Quarterback of your team!

While writing and researching this book I had a few women share different scenarios with me, and ask if I thought their men were cheating or if they were just being paranoid.

Some of their men were cheating and were quite horrible at it, but of course I said no they were just being paranoid-lol. Well what was their pain is now my pleasure to share with you to prevent you from falling into these traps.

I will share the questions (Q) these women had, however the answer (A) is what you should do to avoid being caught...

Q: *My man is always traveling out of town and he says it's because of "business". Most of the time when he's out of town he rarely answers. Is he seeing someone?*

A: (I have to assume you have a "Kicker" in another state, because there is no way in hell you would dare fly your "Kicker" anywhere. I don't care if the ticket is $19- still not allowed). Before you go on your trip you will need to outline to your wife/ girlfriend certain times you can be reached and time when you can not. You will also need to make every effort to answer her calls to avoid suspicion.

How many times have we seen in movies or seen real life scenarios the wife/ girlfriend just pops up, most of the time this happens because the guy did not answer his phone.

You will also need to make sure you answer when your "Kicker" is not around (make her leave the room if you have to). Women can always tell by the sound of a man's voice when another woman is around, you men just sound tensed, stressed, and short.

Q: *My man has several different cell phones, do you think it's because he is talking to people he doesn't want me to know about?*

A: While writing this book a man asked me why I didn't advise men to just get another phone like a prepaid phone and just hide it. Sure, that could be possible however having to keep up with one phone is hard enough.

When you have an extra phone that you are specifically using it for cheating purposes you become so paranoid you become careless. You may hide the phone, but you may not feel the need to delete any messages or the calls in the call log.

You may never take the phone in the house, but what happens when your wife/ girlfriend borrows your car and find it or wherever you hide it. We need to get in the habit of avoiding unnecessary risk sticking with one phone is key as it will be easier to keep track of.

Q: *My boyfriend and I were engaged to be married and just out of the blue one day he said he still wanted to be in a relationship with me, but he wanted to take it slow and wait on the wedding. Do you think this is because he is cheating on me?*

A: If you have learned anything from this book I hope you learned nothing should be done "out of the blue". We need to make sure we plan and start dropping subtle hints if this is the case, if you don't you will look guilty every time.

Women don't ever want to admit it was because of the 100 pounds they gained, or because they were too damn bossy (or just them being them) was the reason you have changed your mind, immediately they assume it's because of another woman.

Now if the wedding is off, that fine, but make sure this has nothing to do with your "Kicker". While on this topic I need to say again "NEVER LEAVE YOUR WIFE/ GIRLFRIEND FOR YOUR "KICKER".

If you do decided to leave your wife/ girlfriend, find a new wife/ girlfriend but never upgrade your "Kicker" to your team. For one- your "Kicker" knows all of your plays, and for two- in professional football kickers are not moved to other positions. Why?? Because that is not what they were made for! They only know how to do one thing… and that one thing is kick, so no matter how good of a "Kicker" you believe you have, never fool yourself into believing they could ever do anything else.

(FYI- and if professional football ain't doing it, there is no reason for you to)

Q: *My man spends a lot of time with his baby's mother/ ex girlfriend. Do you think they still have something going on?*

A: Remember your "Kicker" has to be someone who has no connections with your wife/girlfriend or home life. Past relationship should not be considered as these are too dangerous. I know it will be easy to receive sexual invitations from these types (i.e.-ex's/ baby momma) however use your "Kicker" instead as it will save you a lot of trouble.

Q: *My husband/ boyfriend is always accusing me of cheating. Is this because he is guilty his self?*

A: This has always been a big red flag for women. The minute you accuse your wife/ girlfriend of cheating you have just shifted all attention to yourself. It will be easy to assume your wife/girlfriend is cheating because you will be by this point (thanks to this guide) getting away with it quite well. It is important that you not accuse or question, instead if you feel there is the slightest chance she could be cheating use this guide as a tool to find out.

If you do discover your wife/girlfriend is cheating, end the relationship immediately. You are the Quarterback of your team, and while it is expected for you to play all over the field, this is not allowed or tolerated from her.

Q: *My man's cell phone is always locked and/or on vibrate. Does this mean he is trying to hide something?*

A: You need to get in the habit of diverting attention not attracting it. Locking your phone, keeping your phone on vibrate is very suspicious to many women. You will need to follow the phones rules, however most importantly you will need to demand respect!

Your wife/girlfriend has no business with your phone period. You are not a child and should not be governed like one. You are a man and you need to remind her of this.

If she does not trust you to the point that she is bold enough to dig through your phone- LEAVE HER! Maybe not permanently (the first time she does it) but enough to let her know you demand respect and that you mean business.

Now I am not staying to be careless and leave your phone lying around, however I am saying she should know better. She should know better because with love comes trust, if not- why be in a relationship with you in the first place!

Throughout the pages of this guide I have tried to prepare you for some of the most common situations and scenarios. I may not have been able to speak to all of them, however what I have shared should enable you to be able to cheat and actually get away with it.

Remember…

I. You are the **STAR *Quarterback***
II. This is your team
III. When you find her, *she* is your "Kicker"
IV. And never ever hit the field without your suit (condom)

Now what are you waiting for…**IT'S TIME TO HIT THE FIELD AND WIN THIS GAME!!! HIKE!!!**

Acknowledgement/ Thanks

I am sure many of you would assume the reason I wrote this book was because I was jaded and angry, so I am sure you were expecting me to thank every sorry son of a bitch who ever cheated on me however this is not the case...

I would like to first and foremost thank God, for all of the many, many, blessings you have bestowed upon me and mine.

Mommy- words can not describe what everyday feels like knowing you are no longer physically here with me. I now must continue to struggle through this Hell, as you- God's angel has finally been allowed to return back to heaven where you have always belonged! I will see you soon.

To the illest singer/ dancer, this world never did know what a terrible lost for them- Sayla- I am sure your sweet melodies will have sick patients smiling all around the world.

(Finally a place where you will be able to sing all day without being chased...lol)

To my two most favorite people in this world "saifai", you are the reason I do what I do each and every day- always remember these words "if it don't count, don't count on me"(thanks EJ for teaching me that!) make sure each and every single thing you do in this life counts!!

I can't forget to thank all of the hundreds and I do mean hundreds of men and women who kept reminding me why it was so important to put this book out, by asking me when they could buy a copy. It was because of all of you I was able to defy the "hate" and get this done!- lol.

Special Thanks to the Tom Joyner Morning show- for believing I had a book worth discussing, and allowing me to share it with your listeners. Your listeners truly helped me to prepare for the whirl wind that was sure to come.

Last but not least I have to thank all of the women who shared their input...Mom, la, b, cc, tater, and the 100 women who took surveys to assist in my research. I really appreciate your time, energy, and input!!

There's only one thing left to say "its happenin' baby doll, it's happenin"...ha!

~*Viva España* con amor,
Seis grande ~

www.ingramcontent.com/pod-product-compliance
Lightning Source LLC
LaVergne TN
LVHW021512080426
835509LV00018B/2492